Presents

Kerry Burton-Galley
is a writer, artist, and animal rights activist.
She lives with her husband, Nigel,
and their Thai rescue dog,
nestled between the Moors and the Dales.

What the Rainforests Would Tell You

rainforest facts for kind and curious little minds

Copyright © 2025 Kerry Burton-Galley
Copyright © 3 Gargoyles Publishing
Cover image and illustrations
Copyright © Kerry Burton-Galley

The right of Kerry Burton-Galley to be identified as the author
of this work has been asserted by her in accordance
with section 77 and 78 of the Copyright,
Designs and Patents Act, 1988.
All rights reserved.

No part of this publication may be reproduced or transmitted
or utilized in any form or by any means
(electronic, mechanical, photocopying or otherwise)
without permission in writing from the publisher.

ISBN: 978-1-0684629-3-1

FACT
Sloths Help Trees!
Green algae grows on a sloth's fur — when it falls off, it feeds the soil below. So sloths are a bit like slow-moving plant pots!

FACT
Gorillas Make Forest Highways!

As gorillas move through the rainforest, they push through plants and bend branches — making hidden trails that other animals can use too! Their paths help creatures big and small find food, water, and safe places to hide.

FACT

The Rainforest is Home to Ancient Creatures!

From tree-top lizards to slithering snakes, the rainforest is filled with reptiles that have been around for millions of years — even before humans existed!

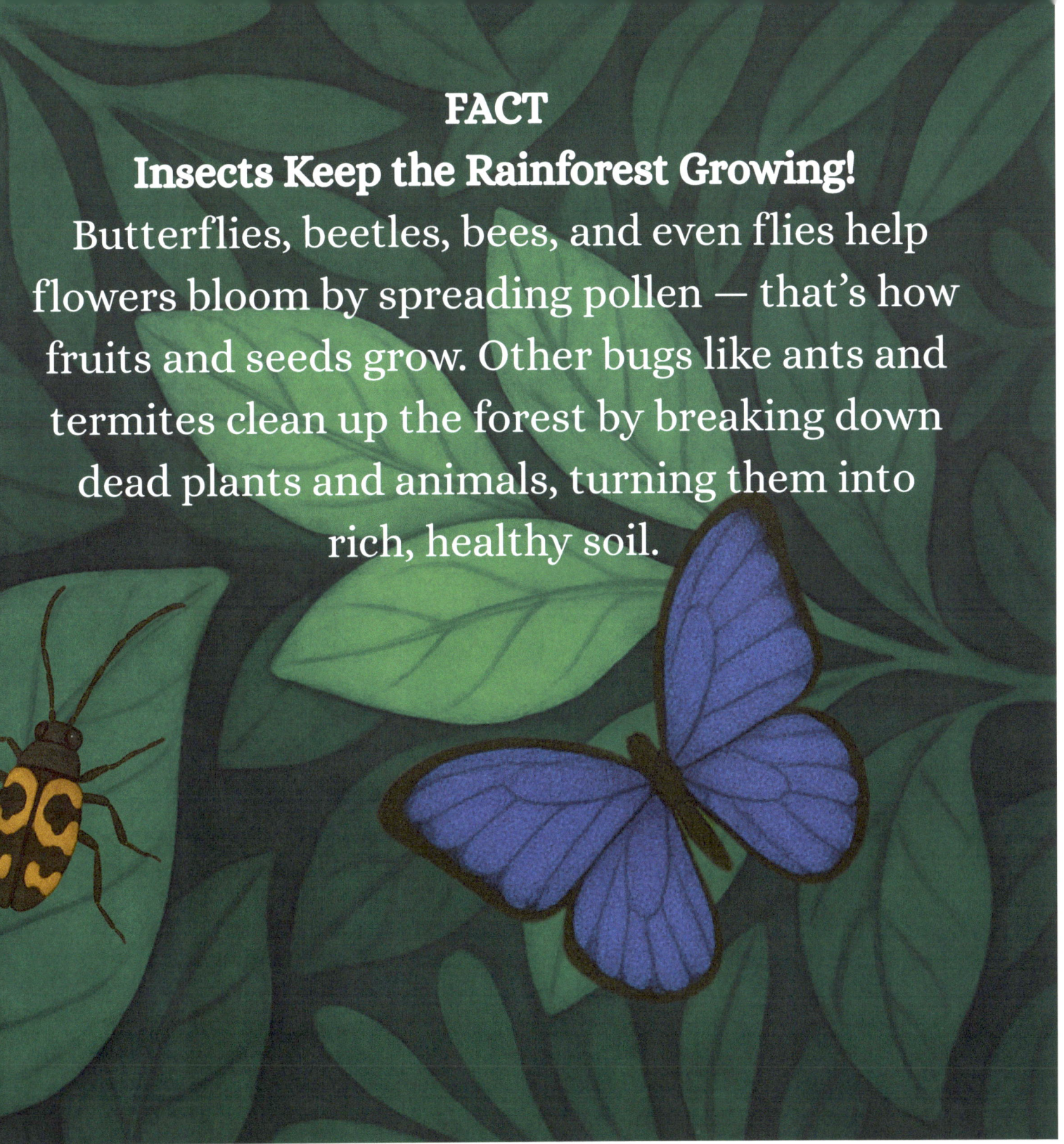

FACT
Insects Keep the Rainforest Growing!

Butterflies, beetles, bees, and even flies help flowers bloom by spreading pollen — that's how fruits and seeds grow. Other bugs like ants and termites clean up the forest by breaking down dead plants and animals, turning them into rich, healthy soil.

FACT
Ants Are Tiny Tree Protectors!

Some trees have a special deal with ants. The tree gives them food and a cosy place to live, and the ants say thank you by chasing away hungry bugs and even cut back vines that try to climb the tree. It's like having your very own ant army to keep you safe!

PROBLEM
Losing Trees Makes the Earth Too Hot!

Rainforests help keep the planet cool by soaking up harmful gases. When we cut them down, it speeds up climate change — and that hurts animals, people, and our weather.

WHAT CAN WE DO TO HELP?
Be a Friend to the Forest!

Plant a tree where you're allowed, or help protect one that's already there. Learn why rainforests matter, and gently teach others too — even grown-ups. When we stand up for the trees, we stand up for animals and for the Earth we all share.

PROBLEM
Rainforests Are Being Cut Down So People Can Eat Meat!

Every second, 1–2 acres of rainforest are lost — mostly to make space for cows and to grow the food they eat. That means fewer trees, fewer homes for animals, and less clean air for everyone.

WHAT CAN WE DO TO HELP?
Eat More Plants!

Eating things like vegan burgers instead of meat ones helps save trees, water, and animals. Choosing these kinder meals helps protect the rainforest and all the creatures who call it home.

WHAT CAN WE DO TO HELP?
Make Rainforest-Friendly Choices!
We can help protect animals by saving the places they live. That means choosing rainforest-friendly products, eating more plants, planting trees, and sharing what we know.

FACT
Rainforests Help Us All Breathe!
Rainforest trees soak up carbon dioxide (a gas that makes Earth too hot) and give out fresh oxygen — the air we all breathe!

FACT
Frogs Are Forest Alarms!
Frogs have delicate skin that soaks up everything around them — even tiny bits of pollution. If frogs start to vanish, it's a warning sign that the forest isn't feeling well. When frogs are happy, the rainforest is healthy too!

FACT
Spiders and Scorpions Keep the Balance!
Spiders and scorpions might look scary, but they're essential to the rainforest. By eating insects like mosquitoes and flies, they stop them from taking over — helping the whole forest stay healthy and full of life.

FACT
Rainforests Help Balance the Weather!
Rainforests affect wind, clouds, and rainfall all over the world. Without them, weather would get more wild and unpredictable.

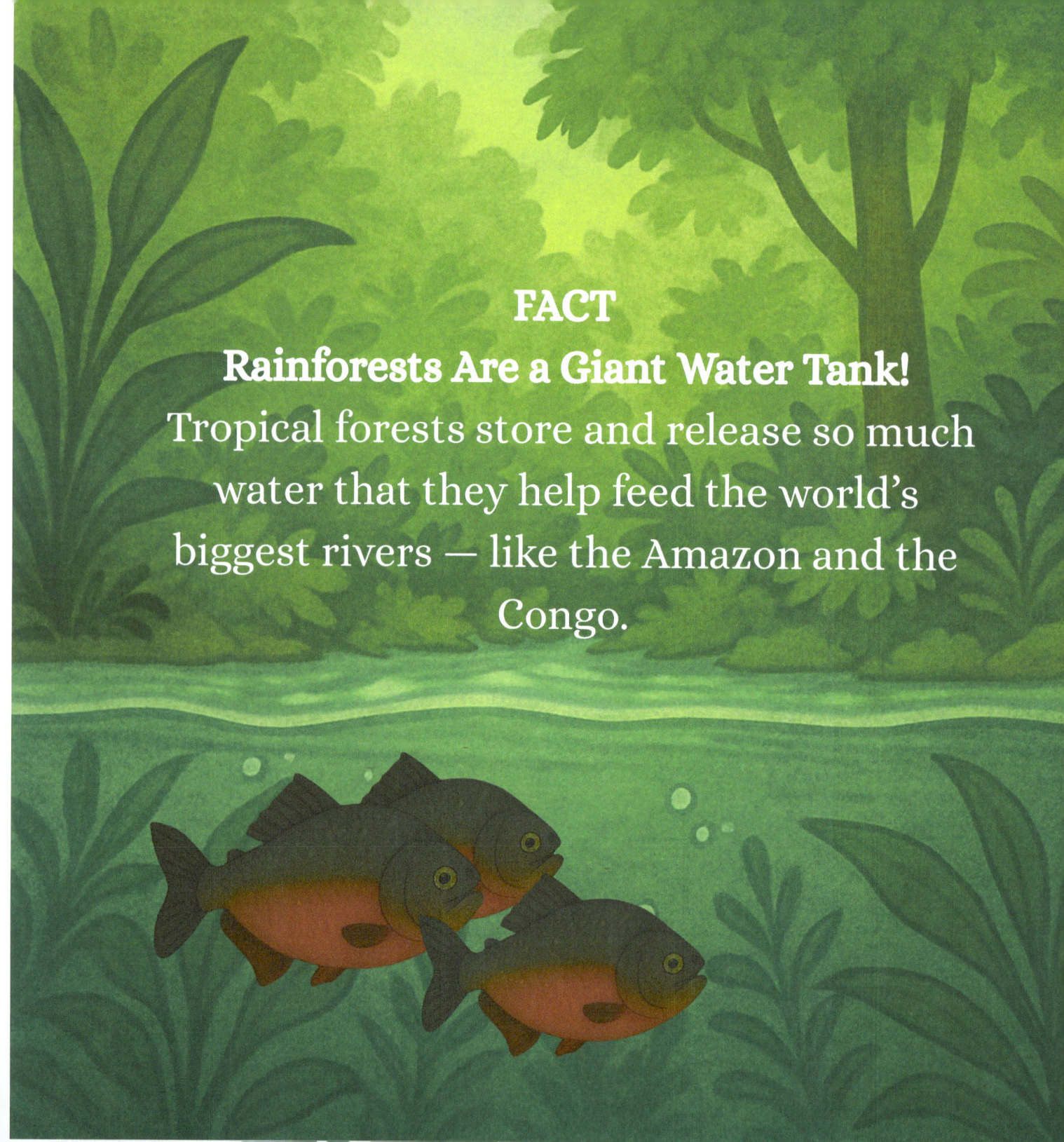

FACT
Rainforests Are a Giant Water Tank!
Tropical forests store and release so much water that they help feed the world's biggest rivers — like the Amazon and the Congo.

FACT
Animals Plant Seeds!
When parrots and other animals eat fruit, they drop seeds in new places — helping trees grow in more spots.

Thank You for Helping the Rainforest!

50p from every book you buy will go to help real-life rainforest protectors —
Mighty Earth!
They campaign to stop big companies from cutting down forests for meat and animal feed, helping to save trees, protect animals, and fight climate change.

By choosing this book, you've already helped make a difference — thank you for being a rainforest hero!

ACKNOWLEDGEMENTS

Mama, you grew my love for animals and wild places. You let me bring home bugs and you never once laughed at my big heart. Even when life was hard, you made sure I had the space to wonder, to care, to draw, to write, and to dream.

You worked so much, gave so much, and asked for nothing. This book is for you, who taught me to be gentle with the smallest lives — and bold enough to protect them.

You grew the roots of everything I am.

www.ingramcontent.com/pod-product-compliance
Lightning Source LLC
Chambersburg PA
CBHW041444010526
44119CB00043B/495